OFF DUTY!

Bletchley Park Outstation
Gayhurst Manor

OFF DUTY!

BLETCHLEY PARK OUTSTATION
GAYHURST MANOR

by

ANNE LEWIS-SMITH

TRAETH PUBLICATIONS
PEN FFORDD, NEWPORT, PEMBROKESHIRE, SA42 0QT

FOREWORD

Admiral Sir James Burnell-Nugent KCB CBE
Commander-in-Chief Fleet

This is a charming and amusingly illustrated account by Anne Lewis-Smith of the all-important off-duty time that kept people hopeful during the gloomier moments of World War II. And this was no ordinary group of people. These were members of the Womens Royal Naval Service (WRNS) famously known as Wrens -- working 'behind the scenes' with Bletchley Park.

This short book offers glimpses of the First Sea Lord, Eleanor Roosevelt and Glen Miller, as well as "Passion Killers" and insubordination on the parade ground. It is a fascinating insight into what made young women tick at a most challenging time in their lives.

But that is not all. This social history serves as a tribute to thousands of Wrens who "freed a man for the Fleet", especially those in Top Secret work. Their contribution was significant and often unsung. Although a few years have passed, I add my personal thanks and congratulations for all their achievements.

James Burnell-Nugent

I wrote this book for two reasons …

Firstly, I found two full sketch books I had drawn during the time I was a Wren – many more than are shown here. At that time I was painting murals during day-passes, the first being the NAAFI canteen at Bletchley railway station.

I did other canteens and cafés, and was even asked to do the Salvation Army canteen for Service Personnel at Euston Station, but refused as I guessed they could find a proper artist to do it – though it was a nice feeling to be asked. Caricatures of American service men, sometimes on table cloths, meant I was hugely popular at dances – but sitting down drawing, not dancing!

Secondly, Gwen Page put a notice in The Wren asking those who were at Bletchley Park or Outstations to write their reminiscences. I had previously written a poem "What did you do in the War, Granny?" and Gwen included it in her book. BUT it made me start to remember, not what we did as W.R.N.S. personnel, but the life we had when off duty. If someone didn't put pen to paper it would all be lost.

I doubt if any of us is under eighty, but hope this will jog their memories of the fun we had in the middle of the horrors of war.

ISBN
1898368 02 3
9781898368021

© Anne Lewis-Smith 2006

The right of Anne Lewis-Smith to be identified as the author and
illustrator of this work has been asserted with the Copyrights, Designs
and Patents Act, 1988.

British Library Cataloguing-in-Publication-Data.
A catalogue record for the book is available from the
British Library

All rights reserved. No part of this publication may be reproduced,
stored on a retrieval system, or transmitted, in any form or by any means,
without prior permission of the publishers.

Collections of Poetry by the Author

The Beginning, 1964. The Seventh Bridge, 1965, Flesh and
Flowers, 1967 (three impressions) Dandelion Flavour, 1971
Dinas Head, 1980 In the Dawn, 1986 Places and Passions, 1986
Circling Sound, 1996 Feathers, Fancies and Feelings, 1999
(All out of print except the last two.)
Every Seventh Wave due out late 2006.

For my husband Peter

—— who did all the typing, and changed my spelling to the conventional, and put everything, including my drawings, on disc … plus sharing sixty two years of never-dull marriage.

A big thank you to my son-in-law, Richard d'Alton, who did the eye-catching cover and gave so very much help.

CONTENTS

**Foreword by Admiral
Sir James Burnell-Nugent, KCB CBE
Commander-in-Chief Fleet**

1   In the beginning was a Travel Docket

2-3   *On 'house'*
Mill Hill and "On House"

4-5   *We usually listened*
Lectures and Bombs

6-7   *Smelling Geraniums*
Smelling Geraniums

8-9   *Hair must be off your collar*
Seven feet tall

10-11   *Wren Anne McCormick*
Signing for life

12-13   *Fitting Kit?*
Fitting Kit?

14-15   *On arriving at my new quarters*
Arriving at Gayhurst

15-17   *Marking clothes*
Name Tapes and Knickers

18-19   *Night escapade*
Foot on face

20-21   *Ablutions*
Not the party sort

22-23	*Eyes Right!* Eyes Right
24-25	*Regulating Office* Passes to Paradise
26-27	*One of our battleships* Ordinary officers and a Special One
28-29	*Airborne on pumping the organ* Pumping the organ
30-31	*FOG* Pea souper
32-33	*Eleanor Roosevelt's dress* Eleanor Roosevelt's dress
34-35	*Telephoning sometimes became exasperating* Letter lifelines
36-39	Gayhurst Gazette Issue No.1 – April 1944
40-41	*The M.O. suspects* The M.O. suspects
42-43	*The hat trick* American friends
44-45	*Giving up my kit* Giving up my kit
46-47	Official Secrets Act Freedom of Bletchley Park
48-49	**Postscript by Simon Greenish Director, Bletchley Park Trust**

IN THE BEGINNING
WAS A TRAVEL DOCKET …

Somehow I found myself alone on the third long train journey in my life. Both other times were at the ages of ten and twelve with a luggage label firmly attached saying "Bristol/Dun Laoghaire, Ireland via Holyhead" and put in charge of the train Guard en- route to my grandmother. He, in turn, handed me over to the Steward on the Irish Ferry. At least, then, I knew what to expect at my destination.

Going to London for the first time by myself, and having to change from train to underground, with my head full (thanks to older friends) of white slave traffic and bombs, was different. Through having been at college in Bristol in 1941/42 with very nasty air raids, I felt able to cope. Ah, the arrogance of the young!

Carrying my case (everything on the W.R.N.S. Recruit List), clutching my travel docket, and asking people who didn't look like spies or white-slavers where was what / what was where, I got to Mill Hill.

A huge building where dozens (was it hundreds?) of us were to be weeded out / pigeon-holed in the next few weeks. My main dread was to be deemed unsuitable mentally or physically and being turned down by the Senior Service. I wanted to be on/near the sea, wear that W.R.N.S. uniform, and meet dashing , handsome Naval Officers (not in that order). As it was I saw very few d/n officers and no sea at all! Hoping, by volunteering a few months before "call-up", I might, if suitable, be able to choose – such arrogance! It was 'they' who would choose.

Frighteningly innocent (as I now know), on the threshold of a totally different life and no knowledge of where or how long, I joined masses of girls outside the great grey building at Mill Hill.

MILL HILL AND "ON HOUSE"

For two weeks (felt like months) we lived in what looked like barracks, though I believe it had been a school.

Straight away everyone used naval terms. It seemed stupid, but then I realised we were all longing to be Wrens, and if this grey building was a training ship, so be it.

On arrival there were forms to fill in – why is it that when under the gaze of authority one's handwriting spiders everywhere? Then to our cabins. Being one of the first in our batch to arrive I picked a top bunk. Whatever ship I was on afterwards I managed to do the same – no sitting up and hitting the bunk above and dazedly wondering where I was.

We listened to endless rules and regulations, and a new language. Firstly we did not gather, we "mustered". The lists (there must be a word for that as well) seemed to consist of endless scrubbing floors, called "On House", P.T., Marching (was it "Divisions"?), Lectures, and an unwelcome acquaintance of the dawn.

Signs were everywhere PLEASE REMEMBER / DO NOT / NEXT MEETING / LECTURE / etc. etc. I soon found out that notices in the Navy are endemic.

"On House" was the least favourite of everything. Our Training Ship possessed a labyrinth of dark concrete passages – probably had another name but I have forgotten, "Gangways"? All I remember is the cold floor and colder water and scrubbing, scrubbing, scrubbing.

All my drawings of these two weeks showed that we wore skirts with shirts tucked into them, but I cannot help feeling we wore ties to lectures and Divisions.

LECTURES AND BOMBS

Some of the lectures were interesting, but lectures are apt to be as good as the lecturer – and of course those given by a male officer had us alert and really paying attention. I can remember really useful words like "Gash" waste, rubbish and "Slops" for the Naval clothing store. "Liberty Boat", the most welcome of all, meant you got a pass to go ashore for a limited time.

Dormitories – whoops – cabins seemed to be huge (even to one who had been at boarding school), probably not more than 10 to 16 bunks. Even so, that is 20 to 32 girls. All strangers to begin with but easy friendships grew fast, possibly a joint dislike of being bossed! which we knew we had to accept.

There were still air-raids, when we grabbed blankets and went swiftly down to the basement. A drawing shows four of us trying to sleep under a small table with a sensible fifth on top. As air-raids were a fact of life by now, there was no reprieve from having to break off sleep (impossible due to eardrum-bursting alarms) and down, down stairs, then ditto to wake and return up ... when dawn dragged into the sky we stumbled along passages towards ablutions and dressing.

I don't think we had any Liberty Boats during those two weeks. It felt very concentrated.

We were meant to take notes ... a useful fact was why sailors had three white lines edging the square 'collar' ... the one meant to keep the grease of pigtails off the uniform ... I think, to commemorate Nelson's victories.

Mostly, I am sorry to report, I drew the lecturers and hoped they thought I was writing it all down.

SMELLING GERANIUMS

We were all sent outside during a lecture on "Gases in Warfare" to smell geraniums, for they smell the same as – I think – mustard gas. I thought at the time that if smelling geraniums-not-near-the-flower in the future, would I stand there thinking "Why do I smell flowers?" or remember it and immediately put on my gas mask? Almost certainly I would die thinking "How odd, I can smell flowers".

At least it got us off the hard chairs and outside to sniff rather sickly potted geraniums. Or could it have been the smell of stray cats?

It was during our geranium-smelling lecture that we were given Naval Regulation Gas Masks, very unlike the civilian ones we had been carrying about for a year or so. I can remember the nasty smell of the thick rubber and the concertina tube attached. Added to which they were heavy!

Would I ever manage to get the thick straps over my head when I smelt geraniums, or whatever smells we were informed about for recognising different gases?

Thank God we never had to use them.

Tedious though it was carrying them slung over our shoulders, it very quickly became totally normal. Without the box we felt half-dressed. Did we get canvas bags later?

The thing about gas-masks was that everyone had one. Even babies had a 'plastic cave'. So having owned one since early in the war, it was a bit like a second handbag. As we were allowed sling bags of "regulation size" for documents/tickets/money etc., I was beginning to become hung-about like a camel.

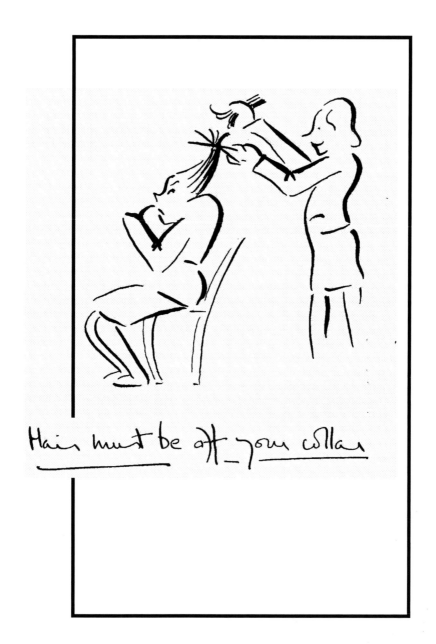

SEVEN FEET TALL

Two weeks at my training ship, Mill Hill, seemed for ever. I thought it was six until, recently, another Wren corrected me. Some time during that floor-scrubbing, parades, lectures and geranium smelling I had an interview about my future.

It wasn't the sort of thing I'd contemplated. I'd assumed that someone would say "Wren McCormick, future Head of the Fleet – Chief Floor-Scrubber – Top Bottle-Washer – Liaison – etc., etc". So, when in that interview the officer suggested I might be interested in more secret war-work, I immediately said "Yes, please".

Then, for at least two days, I imagined myself behind enemy lines (well. I did learn a bit of German at school), or handling secret documents, parachuting into Vichy France wearing a false moustache – until flights of fantasy plummeted to Munitions.

Time does tend to telescope, so I cannot accurately say whether it was then that I was told that I had been accepted as a member of the W.R.N.S. and that my first posting would be at Eastcote … but I remember clearly my delight that I was in the Navy.

I dreamed of dashing Naval Officers (though dreams were the nearest I ever got), ignoring the fact that I was the equivalent of a rating – and stayed that way.

Hair had to be off the collar, but I would shortly have a uniform. Another Wren cut my hair and I cut hers.

At eighteen years old I was a Wren and felt seven feet tall !

9

SIGNING FOR LIFE

I was summoned to a second interview, very different from the first one at Mill Hill about my future. Though this one is still clear in my memory, I have no idea if it was before I was posted to Eastcote or before Gayhurst – I think the latter.

Three men, one a Naval Officer at a desk with my chair opposite him. The other two in civilian clothes sitting either side just out of my direct sight – which meant that if they asked questions I had to turn my head to whichever spoke. I know now it was a simple psychological set-up, but then it just seemed odd.

A lot of queries about parents and grandparents, and as my father was Irish I wondered would they have a bias, though probably the fact he was a doctor evened it.

The final question was "If you accept this posting you will never be able to talk about it for the rest of your life. Will you agree to that?"

I agreed.

I signed the Official Secrets Act.

I was never quite sure what happened so that Bletchley Park and Outstations such as Gayhurst and Woburn came into the public domain. Many of us have queried this, saying they signed the Official Secrets Act for life, and though it may be something to do with copyright, it does not alter what one signed.

That is why this small book is about what we did Off Watch, containing sketches I did at the time.

FITTING KIT?

Before our final postings (which for me was Gayhurst Manor), some of us had an intermediate 'Training Posting' at Eastcote. Prior to this we had to be fitted with W.R.N.S. uniforms.

I think it was a very large storeroom where no-one helped very much and where we had to find out what fitted. Our clothing lists (on Naval Dockets) was two jackets and skirts, black lisle stockings, regulation vests (weird) and navy knickers with elasticated waist and legs, plus ??.

The long list of things (which must have included black tie and shoes) was ticked by the Petty Officer in charge and we signed for them. We were also given a personal sheet of dockets presumably for bra's, pyjamas etc. not found in Slops.

We signed for the most important cap and tally-band – "H.M.S. Pembroke V" – though somewhere along the line we acquired new tally-bands with only H.M.S. on ... sad. Probably in the name of security.

Of course, posting meant a new address and we had no idea how long Eastcote was going to last, and all of us lived in hope of a letter ... in fact we were there for a month.

Peter, my fiancé, wrote the most marvellous letters, answered by return post. He, as a young R.A.F. Officer, was posted somewhere in Northern Ireland. Originally I had thought I could get a direct commission in the W.A.A.F. hoping to be near him – I know now how extremely remote that would have been. Quite apart from Rules and Regulations, I had rarely passed any exams at school except English and Art, though I did get a School Certificate. Someone – parents? – gently nudged my thinking towards the Navy (uncle and ancestors) until I thought it was my idea!

ARRIVING AT GAYHURST

It was a long tedious journey to my new posting at Gayhurst Manor near Newport Pagnell. I learnt Gayhurst was a satellite of Bletchley Park ... sort of 'out-workers'.

Gayhurst was the most beautiful of houses and (despite ghosts) had a great calm about it. The estate and house, both very large, were given by Queen Elizabeth I to Francis Drake who apparently sold it within twenty four hours to the Digby Family (supporters of lost causes, including Guy Fawkes). The present owners were allowed to live in part as a concession to the Navy using the rest!

My cabin, with about 15 other Wrens, was named DIGBY, and a small room off it about ten feet square had a false ceiling – which one hoped was never found when in use. There was a locked and sealed door by my bunk, and looking through the keyhole we could see beautifully painted flowers on blue walls. Several other rooms were sealed, but most had un-peerable-through keyholes.

A long gravel drive led down to the road, about half a mile, amazingly short on Liberty Boat passes, but very long (and uphill) returning. Several of us, walking back one night, dashed to the nearest tree when we were caught in a very heavy downpour. Only a short one, but it left the grass and drive very lumpy. Our torches (bright enough to see a cow but otherwise very dim) shone close to the ground and showed it covered in tiny frogs, many of which we had squashed (and a car following killed many more). Daylight showed several hundred were squashed: the rest had hopped away. Later I was told this was very rare but not unknown – 'A Rain of Frogs'.

NAME TAPES AND KNICKERS

All very well getting new kit, BUT we then had to mark it – every single item, even stockings.

I know we did because of this sketch but have no idea whether we were given blank tapes and Indian ink or what with which to mark everything. Each piece of clothing was later marked PV (Pembroke V) by the laundry. I assume one was not able to make use of old school Cash's name tapes – there wasn't time either. It all had to be done like yesterday!

Later on, most of us had our uniform jackets tailored – in my case with space to wear secretly a red waistcoat. Never to be shown, but a personal rebellion against authority.

We never, ever wore the ghastly black-outs / passion-killers, as the knickers were named, until … about a year later our Chief Officer realised (via the laundry, or was told?) that few of us wore regulation knickers.

Two of our Watches were on parade and standing to attention when the order came "Up skirts" (surely not found in the Command Book!).

A very fine array of flimsies was immediately on show and a lecture delivered. Our Watch was asleep and the other working, so we were forewarned in time to don the navy horrors when next on parade.

As far as I know it was never repeated elsewhere – probably came under 'Indecent Exposure'.

FOOT ON FACE

I think we were all C-Watch in Digby cabin and so we worked on a rota of three watches. This meant one week we worked midnight to 8.0 a.m., then a week of 8.0 a.m. to 4.0 p.m. (nicest of all), and then 4.0 p.m. to midnight. At change-over weeks we had 36 hours break or more. Later the rota was changed, which we hated, worked out by an idiot at Headquarters! Really messed up our sleep pattern and didn't last long.

One snag about changing weeks and sleeping times was that our insides didn't adjust very quickly. It was all right having to go to the Heads (lavatories) in the daytime, but having to go there in the dark was not ideal. Having a bare foot on your face when asleep was no joy – nor finding a squiggly bit of female under your descending foot.

Our Mess was in the old Refectory, which was reached by a long stone-flagged (single-storey) passageway from the main house. It was built by William the Conqueror's brother – very little changed. A high roof, elegant windows (blacked out, some I think boarded up), and half way up the end wall a small open alcove reached by stairs-door (locked!!), where a monk would read or intone psalms from the bible to those eating silently.

We were not read to, nor silent!

This, and the house where we worked,were separated by a small tall-trunked pine wood growing haphazardly. Fine for day watches, but at night, when the cooks slept, two of us had to prepare the meal left for us all. Very spooky in the dark with the dim, dim torches, and we ran (nightmare things lurking) full speed through ... sometimes a bloody nose or black eye.

Happily, having eaten, we walked back through the pines all together, only bumping into each other.

NOT THE PARTY SORT

Coming down the steep steps into our cabin (which was thinly divided so that one Watch could sleep while another got up) I was surprised to see a girl called Vera kneeling on the floor. Her overnight bag was open beside her.

"Look" she exclaimed, "an American friend must have put all these balloons in my bag as a present." Already she had blown some up, the ends knotted, and bouncing around the floor ... odd sausage things. Alas, all one colour, beige, which I thought, as a present, was inconsiderate.

We were laughing with delight, and I was about to help blow up some more, when an older Wren came down the steps.

"What are you doing?" she said severely. Vera told her about a kind airman she met who must have put them in her bag when she was in Bedford on an overnight pass.

She explained they were French Letters. We looked totally blankly at her.

Then she told us clearly and plainly what they were and why they were used. Both of us were horrified and gladly helped her stamp on them – not at all easy! Eventually the jolly bouncing balloons became sordid bits of rubber.

I remember being alarmed at the size when blown up. It is difficult, in this modern age, when condom machines are in every public lavatory, to realise just how innocent most of us 18 year olds were in those days.

We were sobered by this discovery and walked down the stairs and out to the Ablution Block. It was full of another Watch coming off duty, but we managed to wash our hands.

EYES RIGHT

I never mastered marching. Left or right in normal times means I have to think which hand I use to write. My feet somehow had a life of their own, rarely pointing ahead. But nearly all of us felt like this.

Often at "Eyes right" I would turn my head smartly to the right(?) to meet eyes looking at me ... panic for both until we saw which way those in front were looking.

The only really enjoyable drill was when a particularly disliked Chief Petty Officer was in charge of us. It always took place in front of the Manor where there was a large gravelled area. From there was the wide drive leading towards the lily ponds and turning left for the way out. Other minor symmetrical wide paths branched each side.

The lily ponds had once been the Abbot's stock ponds for fish and had a very wide, well cut, thick hedge on our side and quite a few trees sheltering the waters.

There were about thirty of us, and the C.P.O. was making us do all sorts of manoeuvres such as form fours, running on the spot, quick march, slow march and wheeling right or left.

One "wheel" and "quick march" found us all facing down the slope towards the lily ponds. She shouted something which we all heard but ignored!

As a single entity we quick-marched down the main centre drive, leaving her yelling at us. The front row marching abreast did not stop at the hedge, nor the second row, nor ...

Uncomfortable, not good for the hedge, but oh the joy of it!

She did not take our Watch for parades again.

PASSES TO PARADISE

The only way out of Gayhurst Manor was to get a Pass which was issued at the Regulating Office.

To begin again …

The only way off our Ship was to get a Liberty Boat, and Liberty Boat Passes were issued at the Regulating Office.

After a week on watch we had a day and a half not working, so we could get a Rail Pass to go to London, which for me and others meant music at the Albert Hall – never knowing what we would hear but knowing someone would have said "If any Wrens come, they may use our box". We always sat in a box and music was a wonderful escape. Whatever it was, we 'wallowed'.

There were wonderful days in Gayhurst grounds doing absolutely nothing, or wandering round Newport Pagnell (I think I drew and painted murals in the café there) and Olney with its wide 'cattle-market' street (though none in wartime) and William Cowper's house with a hole in the door for his hare – All small vignettes.

There was never any difficulty getting to Bletchley Railway Station or back. Three or four of us would hitch a lift with American servicemen, usually in lorries. One time two of us were hitching together when a large USA lorry stopped and the driver said "In the back, girls". As we climbed up, two pairs of black hands helped us in. It was pitch dark inside, but we knew the ratio of two and two was not good for hitching. Suddenly the black interior was lit by more than sixteen brilliantly white-toothed smiles. They must have realised we were scared and, for the rest of that hitch, sang spirituals to us.

It was without a doubt the nicest hitch I ever had.

ORDINARY OFFICERS
AND A SPECIAL ONE

I drew quite a few Wren officers. Mill Hill had a great assortment of skinny ones with thin whippets and tall ones with short fat dogs, and this wonderful battleship with her sausage dog. Though I have never been sure how many rings make what, I see I have done these plus a diamond, whatever that was.

Once, catching a train from Bristol after my leave, I had reason to write secretly the number of rings on my companion's sleeve. All trains in war-time were very overcrowded (even to sleeping on the floor) and as my train drew in I searched for carriages with space.

Then I spotted one with RESERVED stuck on the window and only one occupant. Opening the door, I smiled my best and said "Excuse me, is that seat vacant?", pointing to a window one. "Come in, Come in." said the man with HUGE gold rings on the sleeves of his naval uniform!

He was charming, even shared his picnic basket with me (never mentioning my waistcoat) and we talked of non-war things, making the journey to Paddington pass quickly.

When we arrived, he opened the carriage door for me and handed down my small suitcase. "Good bye my dear." As I turned from him, there facing me was a semi circle of Naval Officers all stiffly at attention on the platform. I was so scared that I put my head down and butted my way between two of them at full pelt!

BUT I had scribbled down the number of rings on a torn bit of paper, and realised when asking others that he had been Admiral Sir Dudley Pound, First Sea Lord …

PUMPING THE ORGAN

Divisions – that is being mustered and either marched to Church or a service held where you stood (on the Quarter Deck, i.e. gravel drive) ... not a favourite with anyone. When it was outside I always hoped the Wren next to me would faint (or nearly) and I could help her away from the tedious regimented line. Some of us couldn't stand still for long – the eight-hour watches took their toll.

Being "Marched to Church" at Gayhurst was all of 75 yards to a beautiful church built by Sir Christopher Wren (appropriate) which had been commissioned by the Wights who then owned Gayhurst.

There was a fiercely fought-after alternative to Church – that was volunteering to pump the organ. It meant you didn't have to sit on hard pews, but were hidden (and probably giggling) behind the massive organ with its long wooden handle to pump the bellows – AND have the power to ruin the playing ... just knowing was enough, we never did.

It needed two to get the bellows going and then one person could cope, but it was tiring. The organist gave two knocks with her foot for us to start and it made a lovely old-man's wheezing when we did.

Short Wrens were no good as the handle rose quite high – I was lifted off my feet several times at the rise and full stretch, but my partner's hands brought us both back to earth.

BUT – not only did we miss the marching, even more important did not have to sit on hard pews in the little church listening to a sermon or have to sing hymns. All we listened for was the organist's knocks!

PEA-SOUPER

On a winter afternoon, one of our jollies to the Albert Hall ended in an unusual way.

Twice before, when the three of us had been there, the 'Air Raid Warning' signs had begun flashing in the auditorium, but no-one took any notice and the orchestra went on playing.

This time was different.

When the concert ended and we came out, there was nothing ... it was as if we were suddenly blind and deaf. There was a total blanket of fog and all sounds were muffled. Our feeble torches were useless. It was a real London pea-souper. Grabbing each other's jackets and hands, hearing the confusion of unseen leavers, fog <u>and</u> blackout.

Even holding some part of eachother, we lost direction, disorientated and very frightened.

Suddenly a male voice said "Hold on to me, girls." One of us grabbed his coat and the other two held tight behind. Then someone held my waist. It was like 'Oranges and Lemons', we were forming a long chain.

"I'm going to the nearest tube station," he called back and we clutched eachother like survivors.

Fog deadened all sound but I was aware of the nearest 'holder-on' and shuffling noises. It seemed to take for ever until an orange glow appeared by us – the tube station! People talking with relief pushed past into the security of the lit stairs leading down.

We still clung to eachother and our rescuer to say thank you to him.

"It's the only way I can repay people's kindness to me – I know this area well." I remember thinking so did we all without fog, when he added "The reason is I am completely blind."

31

ELEANOR ROOSEVELT'S DRESS

In April 1944 we planned to get married on June 6th. Peter's sister in the Admiralty said "Why not May?" in a very odd voice – did she know something? We did not ask why and said nothing, but moved it to May 17th, both putting in for a week's leave.

All the girls in the Digby cabin were very excited and drew the dress they thought I should have made in ex-parachute silk. Needless to write, I was not consulted and they produced a drawing which looked practical ... "Have it dyed afterwards for dancing."

One of the officers heard that the wife, Eleanor, of America's President, Franklin D. Roosevelt, had just given three wedding dresses, one to each of the three services, W.R.N.S., W.A.A.F. and A.T.S. as everyone in the U.K. was on strict clothing rations.

I think the officer must have applied at once for me to borrow one, because on May 17th at my home church, St.Peter's in Portishead, I was the first Wren to be married in one of Eleanor Roosevelt's wedding dresses with, of course, attendant Press coverage.

We both knew that something war-wise was afoot as, instead of a week's honeymoon, Peter got a 48-hour pass and I had four days. Britain was getting in place for the Normandy invasion.

When I returned to Gayhurst as 'Mrs' (though, of course, still 'Wren') my bunk was hung about with ribbons and streamers, also masses of written notices – some of which I didn't understand (then).

Sixty years later I published a poem "What did you do in the War, Granny?" in the W.R.N.S. Magazine, and one of my cabin mates wrote to me. Among other things she apologised for some of the notices – "Sorry if we were over enthusiastic".

Sadly, so many of us have now died, so has my cabin mate Bungie.

33

LETTER LIFELINES

We lived for letters! Post was left in a wooden box pigeon hole. I was glad my name was McCormick, but after marrying Peter my surname became Lewis-Smith and I had to look in the 'S' box as well as 'L'. All Aunts and Uncles were drafted to write to me, the letters from home being especially welcome: even the cat having fleas or ticks put the war into its rightful perspective.

My father, doing the job of two doctors as well as his own practice, was wonderful in his scribbled notes to me – except I couldn't decipher them (maybe they should have gone in the bag to Bletchley Park!). Of course, letters from Peter made all discomforts and tiredness vanish as we planned on paper for our life together

People, even nearest and dearest, were not allowed to 'telephone in', which meant that, off-watch, the queue waiting outside the little wooden, nearly soundproof, box was tediously long. When I was talking to Peter or family I was as deaf to others banging on the door with "Hurry up", "You've been there too long" etc.,etc. as others were to me shouting the same.

I deeply regret I did not keep a diary, only scribbled notes and sketches, but decided to publish a folded sheet with the title Gayhurst Gazette so not everything relating to the Wrens at Gayhurst would be lost.

A printer in Newport Pagnell typed and set it, then ran off 100 copies which cost me £5 in April '44. I think a couple of officers helped with the money. The second (and last) issue came out later that year and the W.R.N.S. paid for it! Since then I have edited over eight magazines and owned one. Hardly great oaks growing from little acorns – but it was something other than work!

The Gayhurst Gazette

APRIL, 1944   No. 1

EDITORIAL NOTE

To produce and edit a magazine is, as I suppose you may gather, rather a tricky thing to do. I say tricky, because there are bound to be people who dislike the way it is put together and the contributions chosen. If there are any violent dislikes I should be pleased (?) to hear them, and all suggestions and ideas will be very welcome.

Another rather difficult thing was getting round the printer. I went to him trying to look important, but not too important in case he put the price up ! I tossed up whether to try my feminine charms, or to haggle in a business-like manner—I am not very good at the latter ; as for the first, well, this magazine is in print !

It is suggested that this magazine comes out quarterly (the next one being in July). What do you think ? Perhaps later we will be able to add crosswords and competitions, making sure that they are almost impossible, and thus being able to save all magazine funds (if any) for sketches and such like. We have here, at Gayhurst, some very lovely compositions ; perhaps for modern painters the salvage heap in the pinewood, empty tins in the moonlight might prove excellent inspirations !

I hope you enjoy this magazine, and appreciate the many hours which some of us have spent tearing our hair, and chewing gum in order to produce it ; and that you, in your turn, will write something to amuse us.

ANNE McCORMICK (Editor).

GAYHURST MANOR

Wrapped in a cloak of weather-scarred and bitter gray,
Forbidding in its aspect, bleak in countenance—
It stood aloof ; regarding thus the wintry day
With passive gaze, with darkly brooding eyes.
Perhaps it yearned for years long passed, for men
Who loved it in its prime, who shared its pride
In stately walls, in handsome furnishings, and then.
Again in gracious women, richly gowned.
These all had gone, and only there remained the leafless trees,
The cloudy sky, the joyless lakes, the sombre yews ;
Surely there was no solace in the sight of these,
But mere reflection of its loneliness.

And then came Spring, and touched the world with gold,
Embracing, too, the Manor in its glow ;
Thinking, perchance, to make it feel less old,
At such a time when all is fresh and new.
Clothed all the trees with buds, their boughs with life,
Surfeited the air with vibrant song,
Carpeted the woods with fragrant flowers, a strife
Of yellows, mauves, and many tender hues ;

Staged in its fullest view, a scene of youth,
In gambolling lambs, in anxious, foolish sheep
Thought, by these acts, to banish then the truth
That this old house had known so many springs,
Had watched some centuries of such parades,
Had seen a million, million lovely things
Passing before it as the years flew swiftly by.

Proudly it stood, in dignity supreme, in silent might,
Strengthened and beautified by fleeting time ;
None could assuage its pain, but few forgot the sight
Of Gayhurst Manor, standing thus in majesty.

ANON.

RECIPES

Peppermint Lumps
2 tbsp. syrup, 1oz. sugar, 6 tbsp. dried milk, 1½oz. margarine 1½tsp. peppermint essence.

Boil syrup, sugar and marg. for about five minutes. Remove from heat and add milk and essence. Warm up, turn out and quickly knead into small shapes. This mixture sets very quickly.

Chocolate Toffee
2 dsp. golden syrup, 2 heaped dsp. dried milk, 2 heaped tsps. cocoa powder.

Melt the syrup in a saucepan over a low flame—do not boil. Sift together cocoa and milk powders. Remove saucepan from heat. Stir in cocoa and milk, blend well. Then turn out into a tin to set. When nearly set cut into squares and remove.

Peanut Butter Cookies
5oz. of flour, 1oz. of peanut butter, a pinch of salt, 1oz. fat, 1½ to 1oz. of sugar, half an egg (reconstituted).

Cream fat and peanut butter, beat in sugar, add egg, then flour and salt. Knead to a stiff dough. Roll out and cut into rounds, bake for 20 minutes on a greased baking sheet. Eat as scones.

Did you know that by mixing sealing wax and turpentine, you can obtain a " paint " which is amazingly good for painting on china. Try this on your mug (or someone elses !)

ON GAYHURST

Gayhurst's history seems to be one of constantly changing ownership. No family had it long enough to imprint their characters on it before they were supplanted by another. Yet here and there we can trace, sometimes by the architecture, sometimes by instincts, a little of what it used to be like.

The original fabric—on the site of the present mess—belonged to the Abbot brother of William the Conqueror, who presumably stocked the estate with the fish ponds, one of which is now the lily pond. Later it was given by Queen Elizabeth to Drake, who apparently sold it within 24 hours to the Digby family. They seem to have been supporters of lost causes—one, an ardent adherent to Guy Fawkes, has become to us a legendary figure galloping down " Digby's Walk " to escape the King's officers, after planning the fiasco of November 5th. Another later became the faithful major-domo of Henrietta Maria during her exile in France during the Civil War. Eventually the estate passed to the Wights. Here we seem to sense a very different type of family—firm supporters of Established Church and Government—we have the lovely pompous monument to Speaker Wright and son in their beautiful Wren Church, by Roubilliac, surrounded with Bishops Mitres and authorized versions! How British they are, both feet on solid ground, surrounded by nothing but the best. Perhaps they, too, commissioned the beautiful white and gilt ballroom. They sound such a safe and normal family—did the famous Elizabethan maze stand near the chapel in their days, and did their enlightened children laugh at such an antique conceit, and grow indifferent to its continued neglect? The Georgians preferred a more restrained elegance, such as the classical grove at the end of Digby's Walk. The females no doubt took the air there in inclement weather, to taste the iron waters from the Chalybeate Spring. And how pleasing is the little monument to "A Beautiful Mottled Peacock." I like to imagine that the gentle poet, Cowper, who resided at Weston Underwood, walked over to compose the epitaph with its tasteful sentiments.

With the crash of hammers and the fever of restoration in them, came the Carringtons in 1850s. Alas, their zeal for the Elizabethan knew no bounds, to the exclusion of the classical. The south porch and hall was thoroughly "restored," the panelling being ruthlessly stripped. Luckily they spared the ballroom, and the beautiful 17th century stables. Peculiarities were carved outside the Guardroom, and the old secret passages and rooms made secret no more.

Now, nearly a thousand years since its foundation, Gayhurst temporarily belongs again to the King. Will we modern "Drake's Daughters" make fresh history here?

M. C. WATKIN-WILLIAMS.

QUIZ

1. Who composed "Trumpet Voluntary"?
2. What does Q.E.D. stand for?
3. What is a Patella?
4. You say a flock of sheep : what do you say for geese, wild duck, and lions?
5. Which is heavier, a pound in gold or a pound in lead?
6. The silhouettes of what hills are under protection of the National Trust?
7. Who said "Soup of the evening, beautiful soup"?
8. Who was Saint Crispin?
9. Why is marmalade so called?

CHORAL SOCIETY

I don't know if all of you are aware that D Watch, in conjunction with A Watch, have started a Choral Society. I should think most people have been rudely awakened from their slumbers by very unmusical sounds proceeding from the Hall. We would rather like to make it a whole Quarters affair ; so, if any people would be willing to start on B and C watches, they could obtain the music from me at any time. We are hoping to air our vocal chords at the show at Stoke Goldington on the 3rd of May. We think it should be a cheap way of collecting vegetables for the Quarters.

STELLA WOODMAN-SMITH.

FROM THE TOP OF THE MALVERN HILLS

We stood there breathless, hand-in-hand,
Whilst far below us stretched a land
That seemed to laze, beneath a haze of mist—
It slumbered on, covered
With divers greens and yellow wheat,
Red roofed houses — grey blue slates,
And here and there a wooden seat
   waited for lovers.
We were lovers, and yet we stood
With the green grass lapping our feet,
And the little cloud shadows, as fast as they could,
Went scurrying over the bracken and heather.
There were bees that were humming, and wind that twined our
   hair together.
And the smell of the earth, and the pinewoods that huddled
   together under the hill,
And the feel of your hand as it held on to mine.
I remember now, dear, the blue of the skies
Were as clear and as sweet as the blue of your eyes.

ANON.

CAN YOU SOLVE THIS ?

Draw a horizontal line A, B, call the centre point G. From A draw a line at right angles to the line A B and of similar length, call it A D. From B draw a line parallel to A D and of the same length, call it B C. Join D C. Call the centre of A D, E and draw a line parallel to D C and A B, cutting B C at F and A D at E. Draw a line parallel to B F and A E from G to cut F E at H. Call the centre of F H, M, and the centre of H E, S. From M and S drop perpendicular lines parallel to E D and F C to cut D C at L and T.

When you have completed this figure, it should form a square divided into five rectangles. The puzzle is to draw this figure without taking your pencil off the paper more than once, and never crossing the same line twice. A prize of ten shillings will be awarded to anyone able to do this.

ANSWERS TO QUIZ

1. Jeremiah Clarke. 2. Quad erat demonstrandum. 3. Small bone in the knee. 4. Gaggle of geese, Flight of wild duck, Pride of lions. 5. A pound in gold—gold having a different weight for pound to the ordinary standard pound of sixteen ounces. 6. Malvern Hills. 7. The mock turtle in "Alice in Wonderland." 8. The Patron Saint of Shoemakers. 9. It was first made by Mary, Queen of Scots' French cook when she was ill. Thus Marie a malade—eventually becoming marmalade.

THE M.O. SUSPECTS

Our Medical Officer, also in charge of three other W.R.N.S. establishments, specialised in gynaecology. In theory good, in practice our problems were more sniffles, headaches and aches from repetitive posture.

I was in the ablution block having a bath when I overheard the M.O. talking to a girl we all knew as Blossom. Blossom had, to her immense surprise, suddenly given birth to a baby, nearly full term, on the lavatory. Hearing the M.O.'s questions and the answers I believed her – she was not all that bright and I think was one of the stewards. We were all thrilled to have a baby girl at Gayhurst, but alas, mother and daughter were soon removed … the baby would be sixty three now!

Buses would come and fetch us to dances at various Airforce bases in the area, and the U.S.A.F. came to Gayhurst bringing their dance bands. I spent most of my time drawing caricatures of airmen rather than dancing. Also at that time I was painting murals (on days off) at canteens including a N.A.A.F.I. and Bletchley railway station. The latter was hugely enjoyable because of the many service men/women coming in for cuppas and chatting me up!

After a very good party at one of the U.S.A. bases I felt extremely ill the next day (I didn't drink) and reported to Sick Bay – nothing wrong. Went on watch at midnight and felt worse with grim pains (No – not like Blossom!). The C.P.O. who disliked me intensely (mutual) would not let me go back to the cabin and eventually I collapsed.

When I regained consciousness I was in a small Naval hospital with Peter there – it was that bad. Then, after three weeks, I went home on sick leave.

AMERICAN FRIENDS

Gayhurst Manor was, I am sure, the nicest of all postings to those outststions of Bletchley Park. The gardens sadly overgrown – I longed to tidy the knot garden – hundreds of years of trimming lost by less than a quarter of a century of neglect. Also hidden away was a little monument to "A Beautiful Mottled Peacock", but it was the Chalybeate Spring I loved, overgrown and difficult to find.

I had a hammock in the summer and slung it between two trees well out of sight and slept my days when on night watch.

A dry summer led to much sunbathing – on the roof! There was a deep 'V' in the complicated slate roofs, reached by a little door – probably for fire or maintenance – totally unseen by anyone EXCEPT Americans !!

In a Flying Fortress they could fly down the long tree-edged corridor to the Manor (at that height unheard by us) and then zoom up and over twenty or so Wrens sunbathing nude. Sometimes we even recognised the faces leering down !! Great smacks of naked flesh on the hot slates as we flipped over.

Americans were fun and different. Plus – a very big plus, this – they had Glen Miller and his Band who often came to Gayhurst to play for dances, bringing a full quota of airmen. We knew it was terrific music, but not until years after did I realise just how good.

On one of these occasions it was stuffy inside and the American with whom I was dancing suggested we went outside to cool off. In the darkness he put his arm around my shoulder and I immediately removed it. "Honey," he said, "that ain't the hand you have to watch." I shot back indoors!

GIVING UP MY KIT

Oddly enough, there were very few changes in our cabin during the year and a half I was there. Wrens in this job seemed to stay put. I suppose we had learnt what Bletchley needed and we were not qualified for any other W.R.N.S. work ... besides, we enjoyed the difference.

It also gave us a certain cachet to answer "Sorry, we are not allowed to divulge anything about our work".

A couple of times, groups of us were taken to small factories making smaller components (of heaven knows what) to tell workers how vital their work was to the Navy ... a sort of P.R. thing.

In January 1945 my knees were giving me a lot of pain and a certain lack of mobility. So when on leave, my doctor Father took me to a specialist in knees in Bristol who was extremely worried and wrote to 'the authorities' to the effect that, unless I left the Service and had alarming sorts of treatments, I could be permanently crippled. (Luckily I never saw this letter.)

Later that month, a Naval specialist examined my knees and agreed with the Bristol one and recommended I be invalided out.

The night before, we had a party in our cabin – I seem to remember sweet rations being used and smuggled-in alcohol! Next morning a hung-over Wren handed back all her uniform (even the unworn navy knickers which, as they all were, had been sent pristine to the laundry each week) and I took my last Liberty Boat ashore to a different sort of liberty.

I was glad I was allowed to play an ant's part in the war ... and make no mistake, we were NECESSARY ants.

OFFICIAL SECRETS ACT

What did you do in the war, Grandma?

I forget.
Our ship was sixteenth century stone
which once belonged to Francis Drake
(except the new ablutions block
where icy condensation dropped
from concrete walls on naked backs).
He would have been surprised to find
eight bunks with sixteen Wrens who slept
in one high ceilinged, mullioned room
– named Cabin C – where Nancy Someone
climbing down trod on my sleeping head.
Glen Miller and his band came there to play
for dancing in the huge old drawing room.
I jived with Americans, hitched with them,
trod on used condoms and did not understand
– my innocence was unbelievable.
Our Mess was once a Monastery
a mere nine-hundred years ago.
I wonder did the ghosts of monks
fade to evade the sight of Wrens?
No guiding light outside at night,
stones tripped us, bushes and pine-trees
ambushed the path to where we worked –

At what?
I forget.

46

BLETCHLEY PARK
National Codes Centre

Freedom of Bletchley Park

This is to certify that Bletchley Park Trust hereby grants free access to Bletchley Park whilst it is open to the public to

ANNE LEWIS - SMITH

in recognition of his/her contribution to the work undertaken at Bletchley Park during World War II.

Signed on behalf of Bletchley Park Trust.

CAS

Date: 22 - 7 - 05

POSTSCRIPT

Bletchley Park and its associated outstations provided the Allies in World War 2 with a huge advantage through being able to read a substantial quantity of the enemy radio traffic. It was so successful that the authorities at the end of war decided to keep the story secret to maintain the advantage in any future conflicts. It is only in recent years that the true history started to emerge and the immense benefit of the work of the many thousands who worked on the project is now much better understood.

However, the day to day life of those involved in this unique project is much less known. Anne Lewis-Smith brings a charming insight to the life of those involved at the time, the fun, the nonsense and the zest for life all comes though in her book Off Duty.

Bletchley Park Trust was established to protect and preserve the historic site of Bletchley Park for future generations.

Simon Greenish
Director
Bletchley Park Trust

BLETCHLEY PARK

Bletchley Park is open to the public seven days a week throughout the year. On weekdays we are open from 9.30am to 17.00pm, and on weekends and Bank Holidays from 10.30am to 17.00pm.

The cost of admission is £10.00 for adults and £8.00 for concessions (pensioners/students). A family ticket is available for £25.00.

The Park can be found five miles south of Central Milton Keynes, in the town of Bletchley. It is situated in Sherwood Drive, opposite Bletchley railway station. Signposting can be found from the motorway.

Car parking is available on site during the week for £3.00 and at weekends for £5.00. Free parking is available at Bletchley railway station on weekends.

50

THE AUTHOR WRITES

A scribbler all my life (first poem in the Daily Mail at age 9!). A member of the Press (newspapers, women's page, feature writer etc.) and as an editor, starting with the Gayhurst Gazette, which I think was the first W.R.N.S. magazine. Graduating to The Aerostat (ballooning). Envoi (poetry), BAFM Yearbook (museums) and back to poetry as a publisher of other poets – not mine!

Ballooning was the most fun, starting in 1969, and over the next 15 years helping to organise international meetings, editing daily information sheets for World Championships in USA, RSA, Luxembourg and the UK – hard work/play. Awarded The Swedish Ballooniana-Prizet, The Tissandier Award (presented by Prince Charles), The Debbie Warley Trophy (presented by Prince Andrew). President of the Musée des Ballons, France, for ten years. Also the Dorothy Tutin Award for services to poetry.

Three children, 9 grandchildren plus their husbands, wives and partners, add up to 23. Then 3¾ great-grandchildren plus ourselves makes quite a tribe.

The sort of poetry/pen in one hand and a child in the other – feet slightly off the ground, in a glorious kind of life, full to the brim.

51